974   Hebert, E.
Heb   Greetings from New England.

DATE DUE

DEMCO

10095. VAN SICKLER'S MILL. PITTSFIELD, MASS.

c. 1906

Greetings from New England

by Ernest Hebert

GRAPHIC ARTS CENTER PUBLISHING COMPANY, PORTLAND, OREGON

P. G. 1707b. View from East Rock, New Haven, Conn.

c. 1910

International Standard Book Number 0-932575-60-6
Library of Congress Catalog Number 88-80540
Copyright © MCMLXXXVIII by Graphic Arts Center Publishing Company
P.O. Box 10306, Portland, Oregon 97210 • 503/226-2402
Editor-in-Chief • Douglas A. Pfeiffer
Associate Editor • Jean Andrews
Illustrations Assistant • Alison M. Morba
Designer • Robert Reynolds
Typographer • Harrison Typesetting, Inc.
Color Separations • Trade Litho
Printer • Dynagraphics
Binder • Lincoln & Allen

Printed in the United States of America

Lovingly to my parents
Ernest Hebert

A special debt of gratitude is owed to the deltiologists whose
extraordinary postcard collections and love for New England
have made this book possible: Carl Kallgren, Marian and Peter
Maronn, John C. Chapin, Jr., and JoAnn Hilston.

Contents

Circa dates refer to a ten-year time period largely determined by the printing styles of a particular era, the subject matter depicted, and other information providing clues to the date of publication.

c. 1910

Mount Monadnock, Troy, N. H.

Foreword

BY CARL E. KALLGREN AND MARIAN D. MARONN

Originating in Europe in the 1860s, the postcard was recognized officially by the United States Government in 1893 with a picture postcard published during the Columbian Exposition in Chicago. In 1898, the postage rate established for postcards provided an incentive for sending greetings on one-cent postcards instead of at the two-cent letter rate. Friends and relatives communicated by means of picture postcards chosen for many reasons—for their humor, beauty, factual content, or to simply express, "Wish you were here."

New Englanders—always great collectors—were quickly caught up in the postcard's Golden Era. Postcard albums containing a personal record of cities, towns, and country life were found in everyone's home for visitors to view.

Although published in the United States (many of them in New England), more than 75 percent of the postcards were printed in Germany during the period between 1900 and 1915.

Today, collectors search for these early postcards, particularly of the small towns, in order to have a picture record of an earlier time. Local historians use postcards to substantiate architectural and scenic images of the past. Postcard collecting has once again become a major hobby in New England.

While high-tech corridors wind through New England, the states still treasure and preserve their historic and scenic heritage, both on cards and in fact. GREETINGS FROM NEW ENGLAND is a grand celebration in postcards of that rich New England legacy.

Woods Island, St. Albans, Vt.

c. 1910

c. 1910

McKinley, Maine. Looking down Bass Harbor.

c. 1910

Maine, Rocky Coast, Squirrel Island.

c. 1905

The famous "Pair" Tree, Peak's Island, Me.

c. 1910

Gosport Church, Star Island,
Isles of Shoals, N. H.

c. 1910

The Coast

New England fishermen have a saying: the colder the water, the better tasting the fish. In warmer climates, it takes skilled cooks to prepare fish, adding spice and color. In New England, such fussiness is not needed. The haddock is baked, the lobster boiled; for chowder, just basic potatoes and milk are added to the fish and broth.

Nowhere is the theme of emergence more obvious than in the coastal collection of postcards. Here we see a transition from the coast being treated as a place of work where fishermen make their living, to a place of relaxation where the wealthy and the not-so-wealthy sunbathe in leisure.

Drying cod on racks goes back to the Middle Ages. Being a protein-rich fish that could be easily dried for shipment to Europe, it was said into the 1950s that in New England, cod was king. Then electric refrigeration changed the rules. Lobster, once used to fertilize corn fields, rules the palates of today.

We see fish piers in the postcards and even a few whaling vessels—the last of them fitted out in New Bedford, Massachusetts. Henry David Thoreau writes about approaching an old man on Cape Cod who tells him he hates the sound of the sea. He had good reason: Fishing was dangerous work. The sea was looked upon as an adversary. We see the wreck of the Mary Brown schooner, destroyed December 19, 1900. The sign tacked to the mast stub reads, "with the loss of Captain and five men."

By contrast is the emerging attitude that the sea is a playground. Replacing fishermen's shacks are "cottages," the mansions of a

DOVER BLUFFS, YORK BEACH, ME.

c. 1930

new millionaire class in such seaside towns as Newport, Rhode Island. New England waters, with their many inlets, are a delight to cruise, turning the single-masted, easy-to-handle Cape Cod functioning lobster boat into a pleasure boat. Sport fishermen replace working fishermen. The youthful tourism industry shown on the cards reveals its immaturity in the silliness of people wearing formal hats and ties, of men riding the backs of fish.

Nowhere does the remnant Victorian world of the first quarter of this century show its influence more than on the beaches. The postcards show people uncomfortable, overdressed. They treat the beach like a town common more than an oceanside resort. They seem to want to get away from the water, and to accomplish that purpose they build board walks in the design of railroad trestles. They camp in huge, wood-framed hotels to protect them from the naked sea. These are people who have not yet mastered today's talent of soaking up the sun, of treating the sea air not as a function of climate but as nature's intoxicant.

Off the Massachusetts coast are Martha's Vineyard and Nantucket islands, boasting genuine New England Cape Cod architecture but—courtesy of the Gulf Stream—a Virginia-style climate.

Meanwhile, fishermen keep fishing, their makeup breaking down along ethnic lines even now—Gloucester, Massachusetts (Italian), south of Boston (Portuguese), north of Boston (Yankee). They are the same strong people, but the sail boats have given way to the diesel, and the fishermen go offshore more. Instead of the spruce-plank lapstrake Swampscott Dory, today's shipbuilders produce pleasure boats with fiberglass hulls.

But the sea remains unchanged; it is still both beautiful and unkind. Storms rear up, fogs roll in. Ocean waves crash against the rocks. A ship's horn moans across the waters on a gloomy night, its sound both restful and disturbing.

c. 1908

CAPE ELIZABETH, ME. CAPE CASINO FROM THE SHORE FRONT, CAPE COTTAGE PARK.

c. 1910

Copyright 1905 by the Rotograph Co.
G 6784 The Pier, Hyannis Port, Mass.

c. 1905

42:—Beach and Pier, Old Orchard Beach, Maine.

c. 1930

THE FISHING IS GREAT HERE.

c. 1930

EASTERN POINT LIGHT. GLOUCESTER. MASS.   5

c. 1940

Newburyport, Mass. - Plum Island Light

c. 1910

Stratford Point Light House, Stratford, Conn.

c. 1910

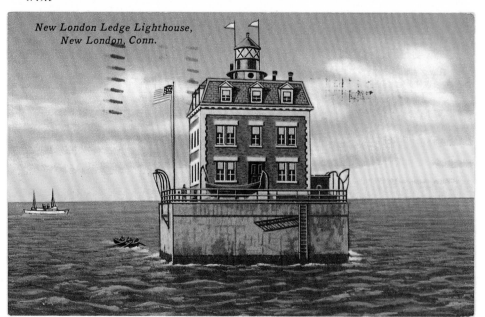

New London Ledge Lighthouse,
New London, Conn.

c. 1940

c. 1910

c. 1940

c. 1905

New England's rocky and foggy coast is necessarily riddled with lighthouses. The first one in North America was erected in Boston Harbor in 1716.

c. 1910

c. 1930

The Fishermen's Memorial was built to honor the memory of Gloucester mariners lost at sea over the three previous centuries. Rudyard Kipling's novel *Captains Courageous* was modeled after an intrepid Glousterman.

c. 1910

c. 1905

Bark Canton "Oldest Whaler afloat New Bedford, Mass.

Rockland, Me, Fish Weir at Owls Head.

c. 1905

ITALIAN FISHING BOATS, GLOUCESTER, MASS.

c. 1930

Fort Allen Park.
Greetings from Portland, Maine.

c. 1910

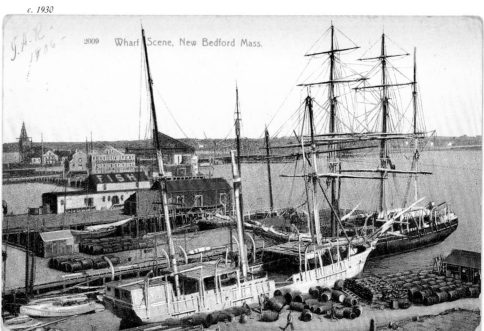

2009 Wharf Scene, New Bedford Mass.

c. 1910

DRYING FISH, GLOUCESTER, MASS.

c. 1917

South Bristol, Me. Lakin's Float and Thompson's Inn.

c. 1910

Fishermen at T. Wharf,
Boston, Mass.

c. 1908

c. 1910

Lobster Fishermen at Otter Creek showing Cadillac Mountain, Acadia National Park, Mt. Desert Island, Maine

c. 1940

Lobsterman's Shanties, Marblehead, Mass.

c. 1925

A GOOD DAY'S CATCH AT THE SEASHORE.

A Good Catch of Swordfish Weighing 612 Pounds off Block Island, R. I.

c. 1945

c. 1925

The Old Salt Shed, Lobster Pond, Boothbay Harbor, Maine

c. 1940

Oake Grove Hotel,
Boothbay Harbor, Maine

c. 1940

21. NEWPORT HOUSE, BAR HARBOR, MAINE.

c. 1925

27:—Aeroplane View of Old Orchard Beach, Maine.

c. 1925

EXERCISES ON THE BEACH, HAMPTON BEACH, N. H.   9

which one is you ask Erma

c. 1940

Sea Wall and Bathing Beach, New Ocean House, Swampscott, Mass.

73645

c. 1940

The New Crop of Peaches
Wells Beach, Maine

c. 1940

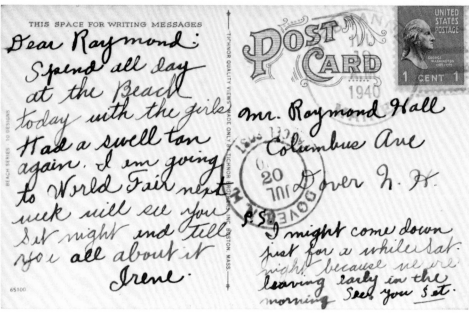

THIS SPACE FOR WRITING MESSAGES

POST CARD

UNITED STATES POSTAGE
1 CENT 1

Dear Raymond;
Spend all day
at the Beach
today with the girls
Had a swell tan
again. I am going
to World Fair next
week will see you
Sat night and tell
you all about it
Irene.

Mr. Raymond Hall
Columbus Ave
Dover N. H.

P.S.
I might come down
just for a while Sat.
night because we are
leaving early in the
morning See you Sat.

BEACH SERIES 110 DESIGNS

TICHNOR QUALITY VIEWS MADE ONLY BY TICHNOR BROS. INC. BOSTON, MASS.

65100

c. 1940

c. 1910

STATE BATH HOUSE. NANTASKET BEACH, MASS.

The Mayflower Hotel, at Manomet Point, Plymouth, Massachusetts

c. 1925

PORTICO OVER PLYMOUTH ROCK, PLYMOUTH, MASS.

c. 1940

PICTURESQUE ROCKY NECK AVENUE
ROCKY NECK, GLOUCESTER, MASS.

c. 1940

THE RAINBOW FLEET, NANTUCKET, MASS.

5A-H2264

c. 1940

56:—Sand Dunes, Cape Cod, Mass.

Photo by John R. Smith

c. 1925

38   RACE POINT COAST GUARD STATION, PROVINCETOWN, CAPE COD, MASS.   95246

c. 1925

44   PICTURESQUE PROVINCETOWN, CAPE COD, MASS.   108018

c. 1925

CAPE COD FOLKS.

c. 1915

141.   BOSTON TO NEW YORK STEAMER BY NIGHT, CAPE COD CANAL.   66536

c. 1925

142.   PRESIDENT'S YACHT (MAYFLOWER) PASSING THROUGH CAPE COD CANAL.   86475

c. 1925

Waterfront, Providence, R. I.

c. 1910

12332—American Warships from Casino, Narragansett Pier, R. I.

c. 1905

Ocean Park, Cottage City, Mass.

c. 1905

Gay Head Light and Cliffs   Martha's Vineyard, Mass

c. 1910

71475   O-O-O-H THE WATER'S COLD!

c. 1910

With beaches, rocky points, harbors, and nutrient-rich waters, New England's coast offers something for everyone. Maine has the longest coastline (2,380 miles); New Hampshire, the shortest (15 miles); and Vermont, none.

c. 1910

NUMBER FIVE, QUINCE STREET, NANTUCKET, MASS.

c. 1910

Martha's Vineyard and Nantucket islands hold prime examples of early New England wood-frame houses. The sperm oil trade originated in Nantucket in the early 1700s. Ferry boats keep the islands in touch with the mainland.

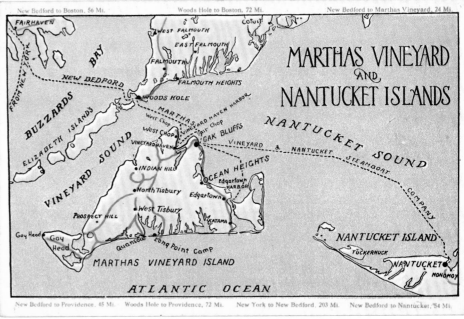

c. 1910

STONE WHARVES, ROCKPORT, MASS.

c. 1940

HAMPTON RIVER BRIDGE, LONGEST WOODEN BRIDGE IN THE WORLD

CONNECTING SALISBURY BEACH, MASS. AND HAMPTON BEACH, N. H.

95747

c. 1925

BATHING BEACH, SEASIDE PARK, BRIDGEPORT, CONN.

5A-H49

c. 1940

LOBSTER CLAW ON THE HARBOR, COHASSET, MASS.

c. 1940

Block Island, R.I., Old Windmill

NEWPORT, R.I. "The Breakers." Residence of Mrs. Cornelius Vanderbilt.

c. 1905

MR. CLARENCE DOLAN'S RESIDENCE, BELLEVUE AVE., NEWPORT, R.I. 10962

c. 1910

S 135 Cliff Walk, Ochre Point, Newport, R.I.

c. 1910

c. 1905

Ogden Goelet's Residence, Newport, R.I.

c. 1910

Amusements at Pleasure Beach, Bridgeport, Conn.

c. 1945

THE POOL AT OCEAN BEACH PARK, NEW LONDON, CONN.

608

c. 1945

510C

DIVING TOWER, SUBMARINE BASE, GROTON, CONN.

c. 1945

SUBMARINE BASE, New London, Conn.

Submarine Insignia

"Guppy" Submarine

c. 1945

Annual Cruise of New York Yacht Club, New London Harbor.   New London, Conn.

c. 1905

LONG PIER, SAVIN ROCK, WEST HAVEN, CONN.

c. 1910

Sea Side Park, "The Boulevard", Bridgeport. Conn.

c. 1905

SAVIN ROCK, MOONLIGHT SCENE.

c. 1910

Tole Bridge, Sugarloaf Mountains in distance.

c. 1910

Guilford Road near Brattleboro, Vt.

c. 1910

Greetings from the Green Mountains.

c. 1910

NEW ENGLAND VIEWS ON BOSTON & MAINE R.R.
"NOONTIME," LANCASTER, MASS.

c. 1905

The Land

In 1720, two brothers, both farmers, strike out for the good life in New England—mountains, valleys, forests, and clear glacial lakes. One settles in a river valley. The soil is good, the topography undulating, gentle, workable. Waterpower is handy. Settlements follow the rivers—the Connecticut, the Merrimack, the Penobscot, the Concord.

The older brother heads for the hills. The uplands of New England range from less than 900 feet in Connecticut to 6,288 feet at the summit of Mount Washington in New Hampshire. The soil is thin. The granite mantle shows bare in many places. Where the pastoral valleys invite civilization, the hills fend it off.

The brothers clear the forests. They log stands of pines for the king's ships. They burn vast tracts to clear pasture for sheep and cattle. The soil on the upland farm is littered with stones, which the farmer uses for the foundations for his house and barn. And still there are more stones. He frames his property lines with stone walls. In one generation, fields dominate the hills, taking the place of the woods that had been there.

That is what it was like for two centuries. Jump ahead now to 1890. The railroad had opened the American West to Eastern markets, which helped kill New England's sheep business. Most valley farmers survived; the hill farmers did not. Heading West or moving close to the factories that had recently sprung up, they began a process that has continued to the present.

Over the first half of this century, whole towns vanished. Tall trees grew out of cellar holes and cemeteries. Today, the stone

Westmoreland Road in Winter. KEENE, N. H.

c. 1910

walls remain, crisscrossing through unbroken forest. This is a wet land that still wants to grow trees.

Even while development and population increases transformed New England culturally and economically, bringing it into the modern world, the land reverted more and more to what the first whites saw when they set foot on Plymouth Rock in 1612. The beaver and the bear, the fisher and the mink—animals once almost extinct in New England—have come back. Here we have emergence from opposite directions: in the valleys, the works of man are transforming the natural landscape, while in the hills the land is returning to its primal condition.

New Englanders have always regarded the seasons as part of the landscape, because colors and textures change so dramatically from month to month. Even our names for the seasons draw word pictures: Maple sap season, with snow-white ground and clear blue skies, gives way to mud season, followed by blackfly season, and, finally in late May, real spring, with its faint reddish blush of leaf buds and green fiddlehead ferns. Summer is lush, almost oppressively green. Fall is foliage season, bright and colorful as any place on earth. But winter is only winter—long and cold, at turns both drab and spectacular, a certain variability in the weather keeping it interesting, if not pleasant.

The Yankee farmer has always made do by being frugal and adaptable, harvesting the cranberry from blood-red fields on Cape Cod, growing the broad, green tobacco leaf in the Connecticut River Valley. In the uplands, the Macintosh is venerated, as it always has been, as an apple of the eatable variety. Up in Maine, on the rolling plains of Aroostook County, the farmer grows the lowly spud. Everywhere in rural New England, cows graze and maple sap runs in March. New England still shows much the same face we see in the early twentieth century.

VIEW AT CRYSTAL LAKE. WINSTED, CONN.

c. 1910

11690. STONE ARCH BRIDGE, SOUTH HADLEY, MASS.   COPYRIGHT, 1908, BY DETROIT PUBLISHING CO.

c. 1908

COPR. DETROIT PUBLISHING CO.

10529 CORN AND PUMPKINS, BERKSHIRE HILLS.   "WHEN THE FROST IS ON THE PUMPKIN AND THE FODDER IN THE SHOCK."

c. 1905

A BIT OF LAKE SHORE IN MAINE   4A-H2165

c. 1940

13231 MOUNTAIN BIRCHES

c. 1905

Millinocket, Me. - Mt. Katahdin

THE OLD MAN OF THE MOUNTAINS, FRANCONIA NOTCH, WHITE MTS., N. H.

c. 1925

70499 LOOKING DOWN THE FLUME, FRANCONIA NOTCH, WHITE MTS., N. H.

c. 1908

6597 CATHEDRAL WOODS, INTERVALE, WHITE MOUNTAINS, N. H.

c. 1908

c. 1910

The Switzerland of America, Lake Gloriet, Dixville Notch, N. H.

_c. 1910_

The eighty-six peaks of the White Mountains of northern New Hampshire include the Presidential and Franconia ranges, separated by Franconia Notch. Rounded mountain passes scooped out by ancient glaciers are called notches.

Silver Lake, Chisham, N.H.

_c. 1910_

10:—The Elephants Head, Crawford Notch, White Mts., N. H.

_c. 1925_

ANDROSCOGGIN
VALLEY - BERLIN

PHOTO U. S. AIR SERVICE   © B. P. A.

JEFFERSON   RANDOLPH   MT. ADAMS   MAHOOSUC RANGE
         MT. JEFFERSON   MT. SAM   MT. QUINCY MT. MADISON
DARTMOUTH   ADAMS   ADAMS   PEABODY RIVER
RANGE   GULFSIDE TRAIL   A.M.C. HUT   OSGOOD RIDGE   VALLEY
                                  GREAT GULF   GORHAM
MT. CLAY   MADISON GULF
         SUMMIT HOUSE   DOLLY COPP FOREST CAMP
MT. WASHINGTON R.R.   ON PINKHAM NOTCH ROAD →
              MT. WASHINGTON   MT. WASH. SUMMIT ROAD   A.M.C.
                          CHANDLER RIDGE   SHELTER   WEST BRANCH PEABODY RIVER
TO MT. MONROE   NELSON   HALF WAY   GREAT GULF
A.M.C. HUT   HUNTINGTON   CRAG   HOUSE   TRAIL
AND LAKES OF THE CLOUDS   RAVINE

                    TUCKERMAN RAVINE LION HEAD

         BOOTT SPUR

OAKES
GULF   TO CRYSTAL CASCADES
                                                           AND PINKHAM NOTCH

MT. WASHINGTON AND THE NORTHERN PEAKS OF THE PRESIDENTIAL RANGE, WHITE MOUNTAINS, N. H   44

c. 1940

MT. MANSFIELD, VT. ALTITUDE 4364 FEET. HIGHEST PEAK IN THE GREEN MOUNTAINS   16-GM

3A-H1365

c. 1940

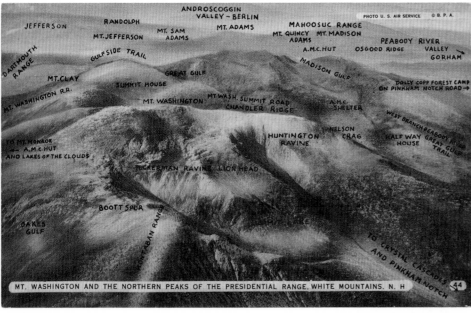

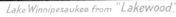
Lake Winnipesaukee from "Lakewood."

c. 1905

c. 1940

Cranberry Picking on Cape Cod.

Dear Nellie, — I hope you haven't one like this. Thanks very kindly for the last postal you sent me. It was a beauty. Love from Pauline 20. 1905.

c. 1905

GREETINGS FROM THE PINE TREE STATE.

POTATO DIGGING IN MAINE.   19.

c. 1925

GROWING TOBACCO—39

c. 1940

S-405

GREETINGS FROM GREENFIELD, N. H.

5A-H2499

c. 1940

Mount Washington, N.H., in Winter

Scene from Hillside Farm
Will

c. 1905

FRASHER PHOTO

© CURT TEICH & CO., INC. GREETINGS FROM THE WHITE MOUNTAINS, NEW HAMPSHIRE

S-501

c. 1940

92—November Skiing on Cannon Mt., Franconia Notch, N. H.

c. 1940

The higher elevations of the White Mountains receive more than 170 inches of snow per year. Tuckerman's Ravine on Mount Washington provides skiing into May and June for those able to hike; there is no ski lift.

10254 BRINGING IN THE SAP AT A MAPLE SUGAR CAMP, VERMONT.   COPR. DETROIT PUBLISHING CO.

c. 1910

10253 GATHERING SAP AT A MAPLE SUGAR CAMP, VERMONT.   COPR. DETROIT PUBLISHING CO.

c. 1910

One sugar maple tree can provide twenty gallons of sap per season, but it takes forty gallons to make one of syrup. A sap run requires warm days and cold nights. Trees are tapped in February or March, the sap gathered in buckets, then boiled down in a "sugar house" (right). Vermont leads the New England states in maple syrup production.

Maple Sugar Making in Vermont—94GM

3A477-N

c. 1925

Rock Point, Burlington, Vt.

c. 1910

No. Woodstock, N.H. The Mummies.

c. 1905

ITALIAN MARBLE QUARRY, BRANDON, VT.   26

OA3987

c. 1925

GRANITE QUARRY SCENE, BARRE, VERMONT.   11.

74118

c. 1925

DOUBLE ARCH BRIDGE OVER ASHUELOT, KEENE, N.H.

c. 1910

Methodist Church and Parsonage, Newport, N. H.

c. 1910

She Shall!

3 hrs. have just got here F. A. C.

Railroad Station, Concord, N. H.

c. 1905

CENTRAL SQUARE, KEENE, N. H.

c. 1920

Up Country

New England is divided into North and South. "Up country" means the North: Maine, New Hampshire, and Vermont. Into the middle of this century, it has been a region of small town greens, one-room school houses, farms, and mountains. And each state claims bragging rights to a big, beautiful, clean inland lake—Champlain in Vermont, Winnipesaukee in New Hampshire, and Moosehead in Maine. Their primary industries were textile mills in the southern parts of the three states and logging in the north. In the pulp mill towns of Berlin, New Hampshire, (pronounced Burln') and Rumford, Maine, local people refer to the aroma on the nostrils as "the smell of money." Natural beauty, hard work, and hardy people—this is up country New England.

The White Mountains of New Hampshire are topped by Mount Washington, by western standards a modest-size peak, but one that rises almost from sea level and lays claim to the worst weather in the world. Winds of over one hundred miles an hour, dense fog, and cold well below zero are common in the winter—all at the same time. On April 12, 1934, on the mountain's summit, the wind blew 231 miles an hour, the highest ever recorded in the world.

While tourism on a grand scale was relatively new in the North Country around the turn of the century, it was old stuff in the White Mountains, which have always been appreciated for their spectacular views. During the early 1900s, vacationers from down country took the trains to huge, wood-frame resorts such as the Mount Washington Hotel in Bretton Woods. Nearby is Plymouth,

Lake Champlain from "Red Rocks", Burlington, Vt.

c. 1910

Main St., Berlin, N. H.

c. 1910

New Hampshire, where an enterprising tanner invented the baseball glove for a Boston Red Sox player.

Vermont has its Green Mountains—in mid-century just beginning to be developed for skiing—played out marble quarries, and the cold "Northeast Kingdom" plateau with its spread-out farms and dirt roads. Vermont is famous for producing dry wits around potbelly stoves in general stores, but perhaps the driest of all was a president of the United States, Calvin Coolidge. They called him Silent Cal, for he was a man of few words. Once, a woman attending a White House dinner said to the president that she had bet a friend she could persuade him to say more than two words. The answer she received was, "You lose."

The Maine coastline zigs and zags for 2,380 miles from Kittery to Eastport, the easternmost spot in the United States. Maine is almost as large as all the other five New England states combined, but it has the least number of people per square mile of any of them. Freeport is home to the most famous of all mail-order houses, L. L. Bean; and Portland, Maine, is the most northerly—and perhaps the most charming—of the Atlantic Coast cities. The psychic formula for survival in this cold climate has always been a healthy pessimism and a sense of humor.

Wilson's Mills in Maine's Rangely Lakes area encapsulates up country in all the irony of its beauty and remoteness and the harshness of its climate. One story of the area goes that when the wife of an old Indian chief died he smoked her like a salmon to preserve her body until spring for burial. The founder of the town, one "Captain" Wilson, had his own problems. He schemed for a rail project linking the Maine coast with Quebec. It never happened. He built a sawmill. It burned. He built another. A flood washed it away. He died a broken man, and by midcentury no Wilson heirs lived in Wilson's Mills. No Indians either.

c. 1908

c. 1925

c. 1910

Maine's capitol, built in Augusta in 1828, was designed by Boston architect Charles Bulfinch, who also designed the Massachusetts and Connecticut state houses. Maine's small-town capitol is forty-five miles from the ocean at the end of the navigable reach of the Kennebec River.

SIGN POST IN MAINE

E-726B

c. 1945

This provocative sign is found in Lynchville, Maine, at the Routes 5 and 118 intersection. The reason Maine has so many towns named after foreign countries is not known.

GREETINGS FROM BELFAST, MAINE

64569

c. 1945

GREETINGS *from* MAINE

© CURT TEICH & CO., INC.

9A-H1129

c. 1945

BOSTON BOAT PASSING WALDO-HANCOCK BRIDGE ON PENOBSCOT RIVER IN MAINE   4A-H817

c. 1940

L. L. Bean, Inc., Factory, Freeport, Me.

c. 1940

S-2

SEBAGO LAKE REGION

Sebago, second largest lake in Maine is the habitat of fighting land-locked salmon, the square tailed trout, black bass and the numerous other species of fresh water fish, affording excellent fishing from spring to fall.

Landmarks of....

SEBAGO LAKE REGION, MAINE

c. 1940

In 1912, Leon Leonwood Bean invented a special boot for Maine hunters and marketed the boots through the mails to his friends. Today, L. L. Bean, Inc. sells to customers interested in North Country gear and clothing.

Boating on the Lakes,
Poland Spring, South Poland, Maine.

Kennebunkport, Me. Town House Waiting Room

c. 1910

North Berwick, Me.
Cleverock Farm

c. 1910

20671—Summer Camp on
SACO RIVER, Me.

c. 1910

Entrance to Central Maine Fair Waterville.

CENTRAL
MAINE PARK.

c. 1910

c. 1910

Portland, Maine. The Union Station.

c. 1910

Portland, Maine., Western Promenade in Winter.

c. 1905

Canoe Club House and Falls of the Stroudwater River, Portland, Me.

c. 1910

Portland, Me., Public Library.

c. 1910

Rangeley Lakes, Maine. Log Cabins and Tepee at Mooselookmeguntic House.

I was very pleased with your postcard. I went up to your Aunt Addie's yesterday. This is a beautiful Spring morning would like to be... you write to me with love...

c. 1905

"CAMP CONTENTMENT, HOWARD'S LAKE, HANOVER, ME. grand daughter * Ruth * From your loving *

c. 1905

c. 1910

Some of sparsely inhabited Inland Maine is near wilderness land owned by lumber companies. Common here is the Maine guide with his canoe and fly-fishing rod helping a down-country "sport" catch his limit of brook trout, called "squaretails." At night, the action is around the fieldstone fireplace for tall stories and short whiskeys.

Caribou, Me., Main Street.

c. 1910

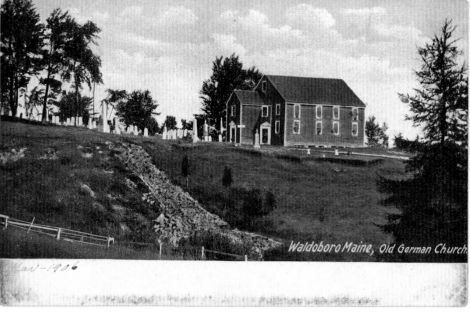

Waldoboro Maine, Old German Church.

c. 1905

Rockland, Me., Old Mill at Highlands.

c. 1905

Hancock, Maine, Town Hall, School and Railway Station.

c. 1910

c. 1905

Camden, Maine. Maiden Cliff from Turnpike Drive.

11082. ST. JOHN'S CHURCH, PORTSMOUTH, N. H.   BUILT IN 1808 ON THE SITE OF QUEEN'S CHAPEL, WHICH WAS ERECTED IN 1733.

c. 1907

PROBABLY ERECTED IN 1770. GEORGE WASHINGTON, JOHN HANCOCK, GENERAL KNOX,
LAFAYETTE AND OTHERS OF EQUAL NOTE HAVE BEEN GUESTS AT THIS TAVERN.

11072. WILLIAM PITT TAVERN., PORTSMOUTH, N. H.

c. 1907

6567. HAYMARKET SQUARE, PORTSMOUTH, N. H.   COPYRIGHT, 1902, BY DETROIT PHOTOGRAPHIC CO.

c. 1902

70840. BETHLEHEM ST., BETHLEHEM, WHITE MTS., N. H.

c. 1910

70576 THE MOUNT WASHINGTON HOTEL, BRETTON WOODS, WHITE MTS. N. H.

c. 1910

13836 MOUNTING IN THE PORTE COCHERE AT THE MOUNT WASHINGTON, BRETTON WOODS, WHITE, MTS., N. H.

c. 1910

13831 ASSEMBLY HALL OF THE MOUNT WASHINGTON, LOOKING FROM BALL ROOM TO BANQUET HALL.

c. 1910

JACOB'S LADDER, MT. WASHINGTON RAILWAY, WHITE MOUNTAINS, N. H.

c. 1920

AMOSKEAG FALLS AND BRIDGE
MANCHESTER, N.H.

c. 1910

Manchester, in southcentral New Hampshire, is the state's largest city. In the early 1900s, the Amoskeag Mills were the largest cotton mills in the world. The Amoskeag Falls Bridge spanned the Merrimack River, which supplied water power for New Hampshire and Massachusetts mills.

Somersworth, N.H. Great Falls Hotel.

c. 1910

MANCHESTER, N. H.   Elm Street Looking north.

c. 1905

c. 1910

Whitefield, N. H. Morrison Hospital.

St. Johnsbury, Vermont., Old Covered Bridge.

c. 1905

COUNTRY CLUB, MONTPELIER, VT.

c. 1925

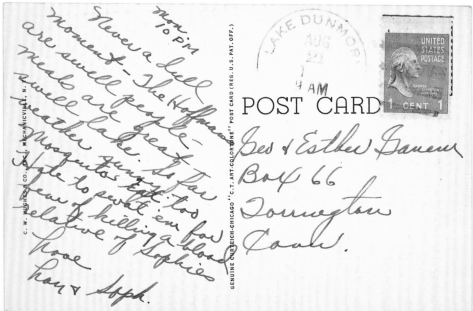

c. 1940

137—Grand Isle Bridge between North Hero and Grand Isle, Vermont, Lake Champlain

c. 1940

PROSPECT POINT. LAKE BOMOSEEN, VERMONT. 11.

*Lake St. Catherine
Hall's Bay, Looking South
Poultney, Vermont*

c. 1940

c. 1920

CAVALRY STABLES, FORT ETHAN ALLEN, VT. 72.

R. R. Station, Waterbury, Vt.

c. 1920

c. 1910

Burlington, Vt, Yacht Club and Harbor.

22183—Ring Barns, Shelburne, Farms, SHELBURNE, Vt.

c. 1910

APPROACHING MT. KILLINGTON, NEAR RUTLAND, VT. HEIGHT 4,241 FEET.

43305

c. 1920

COPYRIGHT, 1907, BY
DETROIT PUBLISHING CO.

12018. THE SQUARE, BELLOWS FALLS, VT.

c. 1907

COPYRIGHT BY F. H. BROWN

POST OFFICE AT SEARSBURG, VT., ON ONE OF THE DRIVES FROM CHILD'S TAVERN, WILMINGTON, VT.

c. 1920

c. 1910

Taunton Green.   Taunton, Mass.

c. 1905

70120 BRATTLE STREET, CAMBRIDGE, MASS.   ST. JOHN'S CHURCH

c. 1910

13267 ASSEMBLY HOUSE, SALEM, MASS.   COPR. DETROIT PUBLISHING CO.

c. 1910

Sometimes called a green, the town common is the architectural focal point of the New England village, providing sites for meeting houses and churches. The lawn, which once served to pasture animals, soon became a repository for monuments and a place for politicking, games, music, parades, or just for sitting and idling.

Down Country

I am an American. I was born in Hartford...anyway, just over the river.... So I am a Yankee of the Yankees—and practical; yes, and nearly barren of sentiment, I suppose....[I] learned to make everything: guns, revolvers, cannon, boilers, engines, all sorts of labor-saving machinery."

The opening lines of Mark Twain's satirical novel, *A Connecticut Yankee in King Arthur's Court*, written in the 1880s, caught the down country native just right. Twain's hero went back in time and solved King Arthur's problems with his mechanical expertise, the very thing his real-life counterparts were doing for the nation at the turn of this century.

New England, especially the southern half, changed dramatically during the century between 1850 and 1950. The area was transformed from a pastoral to an industrial society. The "mill," or factory building, replaced the barn as the workplace for most people. By the 1900s, immigrant labor from French Canada and from nearly every country in Europe replaced Yankees as the main body of mill workers.

"Down country" New England includes Massachusetts, Rhode Island, and Connecticut—states pinned against the sea by rural up country and urban New York State. The influences of these bordering regions run parallel. In the twentieth century, plenty of nature still exists, but buildings, industrial strength, and conspicuous consumption on a grand scale are what is celebrated.

Although much of the area remained rural, the emphasis of the postcards is on urban matters, industry, and industrial wealth. It is

SPRINGFIELD, Mass. Court Square.

c. 1905

a time when people look not to the town but to the city, not to the works of nature but to the works of man.

The march of Massachusetts through time reflects steadiness in the face of change, a kind of thoughtful progress. Nowhere else can you find such a mixture of the American experience. We see industrial might on both land and sea; churches, of either stone or wood, representing the various faces of Christianity; the opulent residences of the turn-of-the-century rich; and the simple, dignified homes of our American forefathers.

On one postcard showing downtown Providence, Rhode Island, a father jotted down a few words in ink to his children: "6:40 P.M. Waiting at Warren for Fall River Train—Dad." This reminds us of a time when the great masses of people moved more by rails than by road. In 1920, the railroad stations—in Hartford and New Haven, Springfield and Worcester, Providence and a hundred other burgs in New England—vied with the church/meeting house as gathering places for local people. Eventually, the train station was replaced by the shopping mall as *the* place to dine and shop, to see and be seen. By the 1950s, when the urbanization of down country New Englanders was complete, the car culture sent people back into the pastoral countryside—sort of—as communities emerged that were neither cities nor towns but suburbs.

Connecticut features industry, city scenes, and churches—structures which were the symbols of might. Mark Twain, a Hartford resident for years, coined the famous—and accurate—saying, "If you don't like New England weather, wait a minute." Despite its industrial bent, down country New England continued its tradition as a spawning ground for literary talent. Jack Kerouac, "king of the Beats" and author of *On the Road*, was from Lowell, Massachusetts. Wallace Stevens, one of America's most celebrated poets of this century, was a Hartford insurance man.

26. View of Norwich Conn.

c. 1910

Great Barrington, Mass. Town Hall, Depot and Episcopal Church.

c. 1910

16688. Andover St., Lowell, Mass.

c. 1910

OLD HENRY WILSON SHOE SHOP. FIRST SHOE SHOP IN TOWN, NATICK, MASS.

c. 1910

3-26-08.

Pigeon Cove, Mass. Witch House.

c. 1910

Clinton, Mass. B. & M. R. R. Bridge.

c. 1910

The Blynman Bridge, Gloucester, Mass.

c. 1910

Saxonville Dam, Framingham, Mass.

c. 1905

1176 —
Echo Bridge,
Newton Lower
Falls, Mass.

c. 1905

2580 — Worcester from the State Mutual Building,

c. 1905

OLD LADIES HOME, CHELSEA, MASS.

c. 1910

YE OLDE SKULE-HOUS, CHELSEA, MASS.

c. 1910

The one-room "skule"—school—houses have faded away this century, but many of the buildings still remain in New England. Churches built by ethnic groups sprang up in mill towns like Worcester, Massachusetts, in the 1800s.

GROVER AVE., WINTHROP HIGHLANDS, MASS.

c. 1910

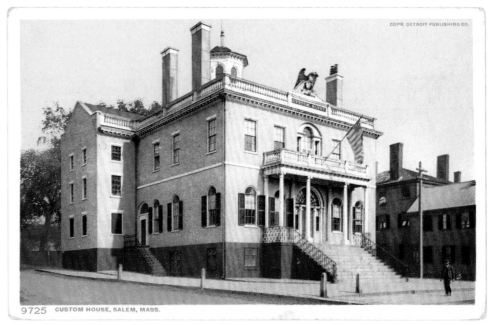

9725 CUSTOM HOUSE, SALEM, MASS.

c. 1910

Naukeag Lake, Ashburnham, Mass.

c. 1910

Sudbury River, Framingham, Mass.

c. 1905

c. 1910

c. 1945

c. 1910

A rough translation of the long Algonquin Indian name for the lovely lake—also known as Lake Webster—is "You fish on your side, I fish on my side, and nobody fishes in the middle." The town of Webster, located in southcentral Massachusetts, was named after Daniel Webster in 1832. The country's first linen mill was built nearby.

Making up Bunks, Fort Devens, Mass.

c. 1944

GENERAL VIEW SHOWING NEW BRIDGE OVER CONNECTICUT RIVER, SPRINGFIELD, MASS.

c. 1925

The Connecticut River is New England's longest river, running 405 miles from the Connecticut Lakes at the top of New Hampshire into Long Island Sound. The western high-water mark of the Connecticut – navigable by shipping to Hartford and by small craft to Holyoke, Massachusetts – forms the Vermont-New Hampshire boundary.

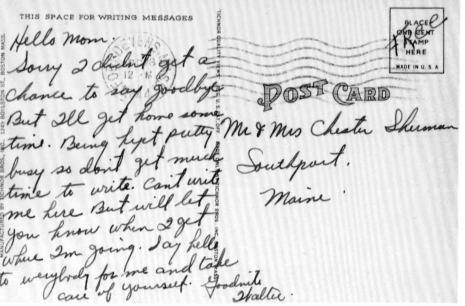

THIS SPACE FOR WRITING MESSAGES

POST CARD

Hello Mom
Sorry I didn't get a chance to say goodbye But I'll get home some time. Being kept putty busy so don't get much time to write. Can't write me here But will let you know when I get where I'm going. Say hello to everybody for me and take care of yourself. Goodnite Walter.

Mr & Mrs Chester Sherman
Southport.
Maine.

c. 1944

c. 1910

Springfield, Mass. View in Armory Grounds.

River scene, Westerly, R. I.

Drilling with 5 inch Field Gun, Naval Training Station.
Newport, R.I.

Photo only.

Copyright 1907 by Enrique Muller.

c. 1907

OLD SLATER MILL, PAWTUCKET, R. I.
FIRST COTTON MILL IN AMERICA.

c. 1905

Y. W. C. A., PAWTUCKET, R. I.

c. 1925

INTERIOR OF THE DANCE HALL RHODES ON THE PAWTUXET, R.I.

c. 1910

c. 1910

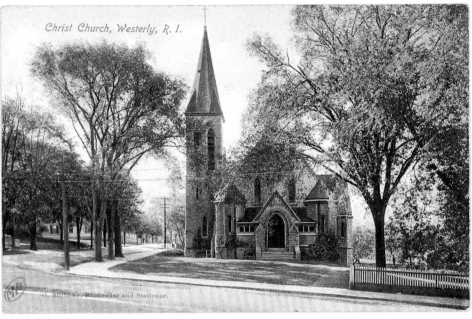

Christ Church, Westerly, R. I.

C. Shumway, Bookseller and Stationer.

c. 1910

Broadway, Providence, R. I.

c. 1905

HOOK AND LADDER TRUCK NO. 1, GOING TO A FIRE, PROVIDENCE, R. I.

c. 1910

Providence, R. I., Westminster Street from Union Trust Building.

c. 1905

c. 1910

Thomaston, Conn.   Main St. looking South.

13725—Waterbury "Wigwam Reservoir" Thomaston, Conn.

c. 1910

c. 1910

Litchfield County Jail (1811), Litchfield, Conn.

c. 1910

G 31534   The Old Oaken Bucket, Hamilton Park, Waterbury, Conn.

c. 1905

LOOKING ACROSS CONNECTICUT RIVER TOWARD
TRAVELER'S BUILDING, HARTFORD, CONN.

c. 1945

Puritan Maid RESTAURANT
CONNECTICUT BLVD. -- EAST HARTFORD, CONN.

c. 1945

MITCHELL'S COLONIAL DINING ROOM — Litchfield, Conn.

c. 1945

COSMO VACCA. GENERAL CONTRACTOR AND ARTIFICIAL STONE MANUFACTURER. PHONE 8041. BRISTOL. CONN.

c. 1945

The New Bridge at Hartford, Conn.

c. 1905

Bushnell Park in Winter, Hartford, Conn.

c. 1905

Notes on postcards tend to be warm, endearing, personal. "Dear Grandma, I hope this will find you much better. Only four more weeks to go. I have enjoyed my work very much. Some of us went to Hartford to see the bridge celebration." (Message on postcard at top right, October 13, 1908.)

HARTFORD, CONN. Old State House (now City Hall).

c. 1905

The Elton,
Waterbury, Conn.
"The most
attractive Hotel
in New England."

c. 1910

New Haven, Conn. East Rock.

Pretty girls,
pretty girls
everywhere,
But the
NEW HAVEN
BELLES
are claimed
most fair:

c. 1905

Congregational Church.   Southington, Conn.

c. 1905

The white, wood-frame Congregational church is the centerpiece of nearly every small New England town. In Colonial days, the church served not only as a place of worship but as a "meeting" house to discuss town affairs.

Thomaston, Conn. Movement Dep't Seth Thomas Clock Co.

c. 1910

G 31594 The Old Mill, Farmington, Conn

c. 1905

If the white Congregational church building represents the spirit of New England, the "mill"–or factory building–represents its muscle. The early mills, run by water power, cut the wood and milled the corn. In the 1800s, the mill evolved into the red brick industrial factory building. The Seth Thomas Clock Company provides a good example.

OLD TOWN MILL, BUILT 1650, NEW LONDON, CONN.

c. 1905

c. 1910

HAMMOND KNOWLTON SILK MILLS, PUTNAM, CONN.

c. 1910

A working man's town peopled by ethnic and minority groups, Boston boasts culture, fine art, and architecture, Revolutionary history and lore. Per capita, Boston has more college students than any other city in the nation.

c. 1910

c. 1910

Boston

Here's to old Boston, the home of the bean and the cod, where the Lowells speak only to the Cabots and the Cabots speak only to God."—Old saying.

Boston belongs to all New Englanders. It is "the hub." We root for its teams as our own—Celtics basketball, Bruins hockey, Red Sox baseball. We send our children to its colleges—Harvard, MIT, and sixty-five other institutions of higher learning in the greater Boston area. We line its streets for the Boston Marathon. We laze upon the esplanade and listen to concerts by the Boston Pops. We browse at the Museum of Fine Arts. We stroll along the banks of the Charles River. We shop at Jordan Marsh and Filenes. We dissipate in the infamous *Combat Zone*.

Boston's streets, in the words of Harvard-educated poet T. S. Eliot, "wind like a tedious argument of insidious intent," and all seem to lead to the Boston Common. Boston—not a city after all, but a great big town—remains patterned on the lines of a New England village. The State House, which looks over the Common, is the logical extension of the New England architectural theme of the meeting house on the Green.

Ben Franklin (that Philadelphian who was born in Boston) called Boston "the Athens of America." The demeanor of New Englanders is cool, and in Boston it is cooler still. Yet nowhere else is the general populace more idealistic, more hopeful that the human condition includes an element of perfectibility.

In most of the down country postcards, we see the "new" New England dominating over the old. Not in Boston. "The Hub" holds

c. 1910

BOSTON. Park Street Entrance to Subway.

c. 1905

its own. Ethnic and racial groups retain their identities—the Bruhmins of Beacon Hill, the Irish of "Southie"—because Boston society less resembles the American melting pot than it does the Canadian mosaic. Familiar landmarks dominate the postcards—Faneuil Hall; Old South Church; the Old State House; Bunker Hill Monument; Trinity Church; and Boston Common, with swan boats operated by the Paget family since the 1800s.

In turn-of-the-century postcards, streets may be crowded with auto and horse traffic but no parking meters. Sidewalks are jammed with people who carry themselves erect, yet move with more leisure than today. It was a time when people walked city streets in apparent safety. To modern eyes everyone seems dressed up. The men strut in suits, carrying canes; the women primp in yards of fabric. Everyone wears a hat: top hats, straw hats, felt hats; and for female heads, bonnets and spreads resembling huge soufflés garnished with fruit and feathers.

Despite being grounded in tradition, the Boston of these postcards looks to the future, as evidenced by a 1910 view depicting life ahead. In actual fact, the fantasy—a Victorian dream it is—is badly flawed. The visionaries saw nothing new. All the objects shown—the trolly, the automobile, the dirigible, the Gothic architecture with oddly modern lines, even the elevated railroad—already existed in 1910. What was "new" was serenity in the chaos of the big town. These Boston Victorians were satisfied with their world, imagining no other, but they did hope for peace of mind. They settled for relaxation at Braves Field, during its time the largest ball grounds in the world. Headlines one January day in 1919 say the Red Sox have sold one of their left-handed pitchers to the New York Yankees. Got $125,000 for him. Frugal New Englanders everywhere probably figured it was a good deal for the Red Sox. The player's name was Babe Ruth.

c. 1920

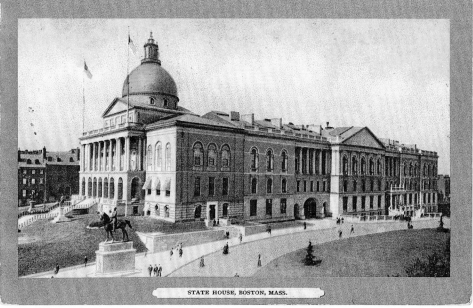

c. 1910

c. 1905

Architect Charles Bulfinch not only designed the Massachusetts State House but Faneuil Hall, Massachusetts General Hospital, and many other Boston buildings. He also revitalized the Boston Common and oversaw the completion of the Capitol in Washington, D.C. Born in Boston in 1763, the great architect died in his hometown in 1844.

BOSTON. Old State House.

c. 1905

2876—Old South Church, Boston, Mass.

March 17, 1906

Just the time I am writing this. Yours A.F.H.

Souvenir Post Card Co., New York and Berlin

c. 1905

2886—Fanueil Hall, Boston, Mass.

Souvenir Post Card Co., New York and Berlin.

c. 1905

STATE HOUSE.   TREMONT STREET MALL.   PARK STREET CHURCH, BOSTON, MASS.

c. 1905

Quincy Market.   Boston Mass.

c. 1905

70133   TEMPLE PLACE, BOSTON, MASS.   COPR. DETROIT PUBLISHING CO

c. 1910

The market areas of Boston carried a distinctly European flavor. Vendors set up displays of produce in a seemingly endless row while buyers picked their way through. In the early part of this century, the sidewalks were more crowded than the streets, and everybody wore a hat. At top left we see a then-new subway station along Boston Common.

70138 "THE LONG WALK", BOSTON COMMON, BOSTON, MASS.   COPR. DETROIT PUBLISHING CO.

c. 1910

Commonwealth Ave., from Massachusetts Ave., looking South, Boston, Mass.

c. 1910

PAINTINGS COPYRIGHT BY EDWIN A. ABBEY—THIS CARD AUTHORIZED

D12475   THE DELIVERY ROOM, BOSTON PUBLIC LIBRARY   COPR. DETROIT PUBLISHING CO.

c. 1910

COPR. DETROIT PHOTOGRAPHIC CO.

9628 PUBLIC LIBRARY, BOSTON, MASS.

c. 1910

7846 COMMONWEALTH AVENUE, BOSTON, MASS.

c. 1910

70987 COPLEY PLAZA HOTEL, BOSTON, MASS.

c. 1910

Sheep at Franklin Park, Boston, Mass.

c. 1910

BRAVES FIELD, LARGEST BALL GROUNDS IN THE WORLD, BOSTON, MASS.

c. 1925

The Bridge, Public Garden, Boston, Mass.

c. 1940

c. 1910

The Charles River winds for sixty miles through Cambridge and Boston to form part of Boston Harbor just beyond the viaduct. On sunny days in the spring, people sun themselves along the grassy banks of the river and watch races between sail boats or sculls manned by college crews.

c. 1910

c. 1910

South Station, Boston, Massachusetts

2B-H1003

c. 1940

COPYRIGHT, 1905, BY
DETROIT PUBLISHING CO.

10106   NORTH STATION, BOSTON, MASS.

c. 1905

STATE STREET STATION
WASHINGTON STREET TUNNEL
BOSTON, MASS.

c. 1910

Trains from all over the country poured into South and North stations in Boston. Up until the 1950s, if you were going any distance, the rails were *the* way to get from here to there. With their high ceilings, the stations made passengers feel as if they were in big, secular cathedrals.

COPR. DETROIT PUBLISHING CO.

70088 TRINITY CHURCH, BOSTON, MASS.

c. 1910

PANORAMIC VIEW OF BOSTON EAST, SHOWING FANEUIL HALL, QUINCY MARKET AND BOSTON WATERFRONT.
BOSTON, MASS.

c. 1910

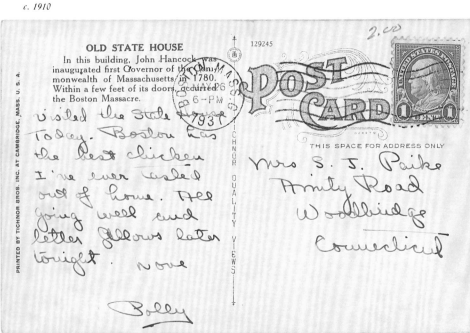

OLD STATE HOUSE

In this building, John Hancock was inaugurated first Governor of the Commonwealth of Massachusetts in 1780. Within a few feet of its doors, occurred the Boston Massacre.

129245

POST CARD

THIS SPACE FOR ADDRESS ONLY

Visited the State today. Boston has the best chicken I've ever tasted out of home. All going well and letter follows later tonight. Love

Bobby

Mrs. S. J. Paike
Amity Road
Woodbridge
Connecticut

PRINTED BY TICHNOR BROS. INC. AT CAMBRIDGE, MASS. U.S.A.

TICHNOR QUALITY VIEWS

c. 1937

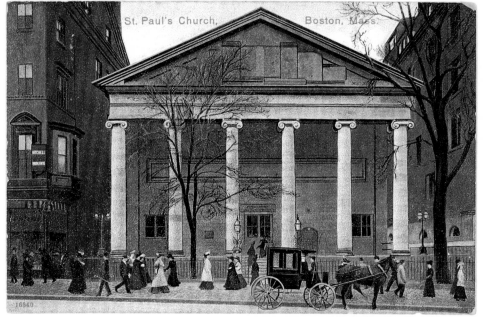

St. Paul's Church,   Boston, Mass.

16540

c. 1910

Cambridge, Mass. Phillips Brooks House, Harvard College.

c. 1910

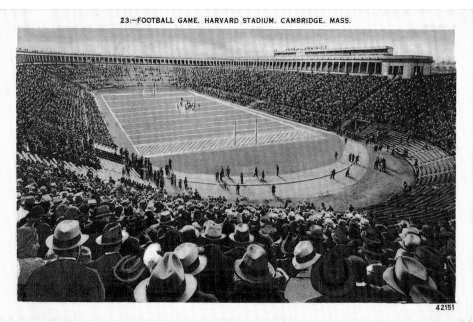

23:—FOOTBALL GAME. HARVARD STADIUM. CAMBRIDGE. MASS.

42151

c. 1940

THE CAMPUS, YALE UNIVERSITY, LOOKING SOUTH, NEW HAVEN, CONN.

c. 1910

Education

Fit youths for the University . . . it being one chief project of that old deluder, Satan, to keep men from the knowledge of the scriptures."—From the preamble to a Connecticut law requiring towns to support public education.

In the 1700s, Andrew Burnaby, a visiting Anglican minister from England, reports that a visitor to Massachusetts soon learns that, upon dismounting from his horse, he might as well tell the story of his life immediately, for he will have no rest until he does. Perhaps early colonists associated the need for knowledge with the will to survive in the New World—the pleasures of knowledge with the curiosity about the Old World they left behind. Whatever the reason, New Englanders have always been inquisitive.

By the American Revolution, they had come under the spell of the Enlightenment. It was an age of optimism, when it was believed that common people endowed with reason could shape the future. It was natural that New Englanders would be swept up by this idea, and it was natural that they would believe in education.

Spanning three centuries, two approaches to education emerge. The first is an attempt to balance Classical forms with a Romantic vision. A look at school building architecture reflects this creative tension. In such structures as the Phillips Brooks House of Harvard, we notice the Classical lines of ancient Greece and Rome. In the castlelike Oread Institute of Worcester, we see a Gothic Fantasy, the American yearning for exploration.

The second pattern has to do with equality. The development of New England's schools—and by extension the nation's—has

c. 1910

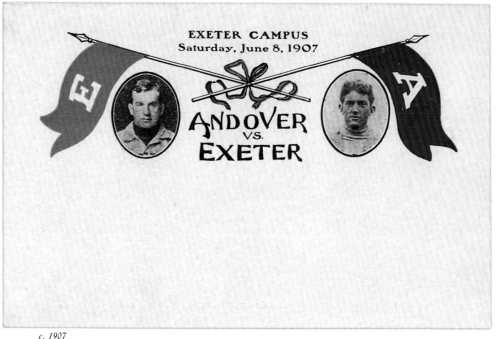

EXETER CAMPUS
Saturday, June 8, 1907

ANDOVER
VS.
EXETER

c. 1907

been a continual struggle to provide the tools of knowledge for more and more people. This quest began in the 1700s with education for privileged young men in the Ivy League schools—Harvard, Yale, Dartmouth, Brown—all in New England. Later came a second level of similar schools—Middlebury, Williams, etc. Next came elitist schools for young women—Radcliffe, Smith, Wellesley, Connecticut College, Mount Holyoke.

The Civil War changed the emphasis from classical to applied learning. Agricultural, mechanical, and military schools sprang up, beginning in 1861 with the Massachusetts Institute of Technology. Then came government involvement in higher education and in the founding of state universities and state colleges. Besides institutions of higher learning, the proud prep schools, based on the English model of academies, developed—Mark Hopkins, Northfield, Mount Hermon, Cushing. Andover, Massachusetts, versus Exeter, New Hampshire, right across the border made for a great spirited rivalry.

Schools outside the mainstream, sometimes odd, sometimes merely speciality schools, also found a place in New England. The Reeve Law School in Litchfield, Connecticut (birthplace of Harriet Beecher Stowe) was the nation's first such institution. We see Bronson Alcott's "School of Philosophy" in Concord, Massachusetts, an outgrowth of nineteenth-century Transcendentalism. Alcott's famous daughter, Louisa May, was educated there along with her less celebrated sister, May, who did still-life paintings. Robert Frost, the eminent New England poet of the 1900s, taught and lectured at many area colleges and high schools.

Despite changes in technology, in social attitudes, and in the ethnic and racial makeup of New England, the region's commitment to education has remained steadfast. Our glory is in our educational institutions and our attitudes toward learning.

Cambridge, Mass., Radcliffe College.

c. 1910

11698. LEAVING CHAPEL, MT. HOLYOKE COLLEGE, SOUTH HADLEY, MASS.

COPYRIGHT, 1908 BY
DETROIT PUBLISHING CO.

c. 1908

80379 LIBRARY, WELLESLEY COLLEGE, MASS.

c. 1910

FRANKLIN KING HOUSE, SMITH COLLEGE, NORTHAMPTON, MASS. 7

6A-H2595

c. 1940

King Chapel, Bowdoin College. Brunswick, Me. *Come up, can't you, you'll find Ina at Vita (Raundin Port...*

c. 1905

Oread Institute, Worcester. Mass.

F. A. Ramsdell.

c. 1905

Middletown, Conn. Wesleyan University. Phi Nu Theta House.

c. 1905

HARTFORD, Conn. Trinity College.

c. 1910

c. 1910

Sculpture Hall - South - Art Building, Bowdoin College, Brunswick, Maine.

Mary Harkness House, Connecticut College for Women, New London, Conn.

7A-H3198

c. 1940

BENNINGTON COLLEGE, BENNINGTON, VT.   60

4A-H1556

c. 1940

HARVARD BRIDGE AND MASSACHUSETTS INSTITUTE OF TECHNOLOGY, CAMBRIDGE, MASS.

3A-H1179

c. 1940

Horticultural Building, University of Connecticut, Storrs, Conn.

69327-N

c. 1930

WILLIAMS COLLEGE. Laboratories and Jesup Hall.

c. 1905

PROVIDENCE, R.I. Gates, Brown University.

c. 1905

THE PRESIDENTS RESIDENCE, DARTMOUTH COLLEGE, HANOVER, N. H.

589-29

c. 1930

D70103 PATH TO SCHOOL OF PHILOSOPHY, CONCORD, MASS.

COPR. DETROIT PUBLISHING CO.

c. 1910

c. 1910

c. 1940

c. 1905

History and Culture

After great pain, a formal feeling comes—
The nerves sit ceremonious, like Tombs—
The stiff Heart questions was it He, that bore,
And Yesterday, or Centuries before?

BY EMILY DICKINSON (1830-1886)

Measured by North American standards, New England contains as much history and culture as does any other place on the continent.

The postcards bring us there visually: Henry David Thoreau's hut on Walden Pond. New England glories in its high culture— Henry Wadsworth Longfellow in Portland, Maine; Ralph Waldo Emerson in Concord, Massachusetts; Daniel Webster with his devil in Franklin, New Hampshire; Noah Webster with his dictionary in Hartford, Connecticut; Emily Dickinson, the Belle of Amherst, Massachusetts.

The words of literary figures linger on long after their death. When Thoreau was jailed for failing to pay taxes on his cabin on Walden Pond, Emerson reportedly asked him, "What are you doing in there, Henry?" Thoreau replied, "What are you doing out there?" Today Walden Pond is a park and preserve.

A mill woman in Lowell, Massachusetts, had a boyfriend named Edgar Allen Poe. The story goes that Poe wrote his poem, "The Raven," while lodging at The Old Worthy Inn.

Harriet Beecher Stowe owned a house beside Mark Twain's in Hartford. There in her dressing room is a vial of arsenic, a poison

c. 1910

used in small amounts by many Victorian ladies because it gave them a fashionable, pale complexion. Quite an irony. Stowe's anti-slavery novel, *Uncle Tom's Cabin*, had more effect on the American public than any other single literary effort. When President Abraham Lincoln was introduced to her, he reportedly remarked, "So this is the little lady that started the Civil War."

New Englanders have always been taciturn in personality, conservative in action, but liberal in outlook. The abolition movement began in New England. Henry James wrote *The Bostonians*, a novel that today would be called a "woman's novel." Louisa May Alcott, another New England novelist, wrote *Little Women*.

So much of what has made America happened in New England, and the monuments are there to prove it—the Lexington Green associated with Paul Revere and his famous ride, or Bunker Hill where the country boys stood up against the king's professional army. (Actually, the battle was fought on nearby Breed's Hill.) At the site of the Bennington Monument in Vermont, the Green Mountain boys gave the British a sample of guerilla warfare, Colonial style. In New England's past, we find the underground railroad of the anti-slavers, Robert Frost and his "road untaken," and Thornton Wilder's "Our Town."

The postcard artists celebrate the first Thanksgiving, showing us Te-We-Lee-Ma, the last living descendant of Massasoit. Today, Plymouth Rock, where the first whites stepped off the Mayflower in 1607, is a tourist attraction. The Native American culture has all but vanished from New England, remaining in the mainstream culture only through place names, mainly mountains and bodies of water.

A harsh climate and a complex history have left New Englanders with a unique turn of mind, practical and thoughtful, one that values individual freedom above all.

Off Frenchmen's Bay, Bar Harbor, Me.

c. 1910

Birthplace of Ethan Allen (Jan. 10, 1737),
Hero of Ticonderoga, Lichfield, Conn.

c. 1910

The Constitution (Old Ironside).
the most renowned vessel in the United States
navy, built in Boston in 1797.

c. 1910

"ENDURANCE IS THE CROWNING QUALITY AND PATIENCE ALL THE PASSION OF GREAT HEARTS" *James Russell Lowell*

HOME OF JAMES RUSSELL LOWELL, BUILT 1767, CAMBRIDGE, MASS.

c. 1930

Paul Revere House, Boston, Mass.

c. 1940

D12528   THE WADSWORTH-LONGFELLOW HOUSE, PORTLAND, ME.   BUILT IN 1785

c. 1910

201:—HOME OF RALPH WALDO EMERSON, CONCORD, MASS.

22051

c. 1930

THOREAU'S COVE

D71341   SITE OF THOREAU'S HUT, LAKE WALDEN, CONCORD, MASS.   COPR. DETROIT PUBLISHING CO.

c. 1910

70100   HOME OF LOUISA M. ALCOTT, CONCORD, MASS.   COPR. DETROIT PUBLISHING CO.

c. 1910

THE ATTIC TO "THE HOUSE OF THE SEVEN GABLES," SALEM, MASS.

COPYRIGHT C. O. EMMERTON

c. 1910

Hawthorne's Wayside, Concord, Mass.

6 417 8

c. 1940

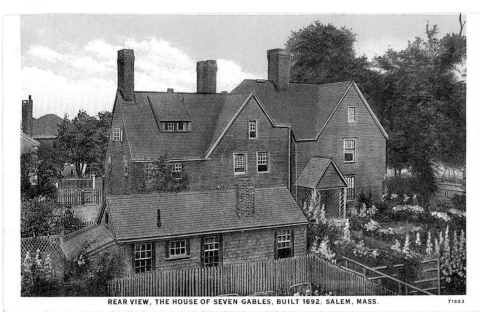

REAR VIEW, THE HOUSE OF SEVEN GABLES, BUILT 1692, SALEM, MASS.

71683

c. 1930

Nathaniel Hawthorne, born in Salem, Massachusetts, in 1804, expended his literary genius upon his Puritan ancestors. Upon his success with *The Scarlet Letter*, he moved to Pittsfield, Massachusetts, where he wrote *The House of Seven Gables*. He died in Plymouth, New Hampshire, in 1864 traveling with former President Franklin Pierce.

c. 1940

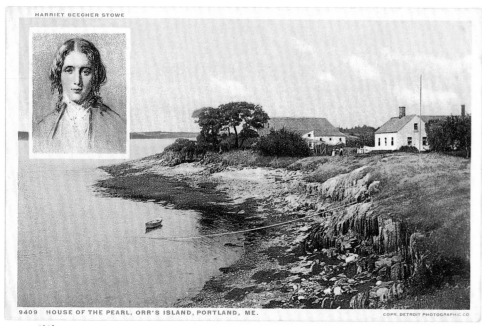

HARRIET BEECHER STOWE

9409   HOUSE OF THE PEARL, ORR'S ISLAND, PORTLAND, ME.   COPR. DETROIT PHOTOGRAPHIC CO

c. 1910

Although best known as a Missouri-born Western writer, Mark Twain built his dream house in Hartford, Connecticut. The house, designed to resemble a Mississippi River paddle boat, is beside the more austere residence of another famous author, Harriet Beecher Stowe. Calvin Coolidge was President from 1920 to 1924, the heyday of postcards.

CALVIN COOLIDGE, BORN JULY 4TH, 1872, PLYMOUTH, VERMONT   45GM

CHURCH AT PLYMOUTH, VT. ATTENDED BY COOLIDGE FAMILY

SCHOOL ATTENDED BY CALVIN COOLIDGE

4A-H2156

c. 1940

c. 1925

c. 1910

c. 1910

Massasoit (1620-1661) made a number of treaties with the Pilgrims, but his son Metacomet (King Philip) had problems. The result was the King Philip War, when one of every sixteen white men died and Metacomet was killed.

c. 1910

2879—*Washington Monument, Arlington St. Church, Boston, Mass.*

Souvenir Post Card Co., New York and Berlin.

c. 1905

D.A.R. Building, Vineyard Haven, Mass.

c. 1910

YANKEE DOODLE, THE SPIRIT OF 1776.　　1301

c. 1905

Willard's painting, *The Spirit of '76*, was completed for the 1876 national centennial. John H. Devereux, whose son was the drummer boy model, gave the painting to the town of Marblehead, Massachusetts.

c. 1910